Americans at War

TIMELINE *of the* CIVIL WAR

By Charlie Samuels

Gareth Stevens
Publishing

Please visit our website, www.garethstevens.com. For a free color catalog of all our high-quality books, call toll-free 1-800-542-2595 or fax 1-877-542-2596.

Library of Congress Cataloging-in-Publication Data
Samuels, Charlie, 1961-
Timeline of the Civil War / Charlie Samuels.
    p. cm. — (Americans at war : a Gareth Stevens timeline series)
Includes index.
ISBN 978-1-4339-5912-7 (pbk.)
ISBN 978-1-4339-5913-4 (6-pack)
ISBN 978-1-4339-5910-3 (library binding)
1. United States—History—Civil War, 1861-1865—Juvenile literature. 2. United States—History—Civil War, 1861-1865—Campaigns—Juvenile literature. I. Title.
E468.S148 2011
973.7—dc22

                    2010049253

Published in 2012 by
Gareth Stevens Publishing
111 East 14th Street, Suite 349
New York, NY 10003

© 2011 Brown Bear Books Ltd

For Brown Bear Books Ltd:
Editorial Director: Lindsey Lowe
Managing Editor: Tim Cooke
Children's Publisher: Anne O'Daly
Art Director: Jeni Child
Designer: Karen Perry
Picture Manager: Sophie Mortimer
Production Director: Alastair Gourlay

Picture Credits:
Front Cover: Library of Congress

Key: t = top, b = bottom
Christie's Images: 26; **Corbis:** 7, 20; Bettmann 21, 27; **Franz-Marc Frei:** 24; **Getty Images:** 22, 23;
Library of Congress: 11, 13, 17, 18, 19, 25t, 25b, 28t, 28b, 30, 32, 33, 34, 37, 44t, 45;
Mary Evans Picture Library: 15; **Peter Newark:** 42, 44b; **Robert Hunt Library:** 10, 36b, 39;
U.S. National Archives: 6, 8, 9, 12, 14, 29, 36t, 38, 41

All Artworks © Brown Bear Books Ltd

Manufactured in the United States of America
1 2 3 4 5 6 7 8 9 12 11 10

CPSIA compliance information: Batch #BRS11GS: For further information contact Gareth Stevens, New York, New York at 1-800-542-2595.

Contents

Introduction

**One of the bloodiest conflicts in US history, the
Civil War pitted American against American in what
became known as the "war between brothers."**

With the nation divided by contrasting attitudes towards
slavery, Southern states began to secede in late 1860
in an attempt to preserve their lifestyle and economy. Led by
President Abraham Lincoln, the North went to war to preserve
the Union. It was only with the Emancipation Proclamation
of September 1862 that the abolition of slavery became an
expressed war aim of the North.

The Course of the War

The South went on the offensive early, coming close to invading
the North. The Union slowly gained the advantage, however, as
it exploited its industrial strength and railroads in order to arm
and transport its troops, and as it gained control of rivers that
led like highways to the heart of the Confederacy. The South's
"high-water mark" came at the Battle of Gettysburg in July 1863,
the largest battle of the conflict and its turning point. After the
close-run Union victory, the South never threatened to invade
the North again. Northern forces entered the South, bringing
devastation and great suffering to civilians. By the time
Southern general Robert E. Lee surrendered to future president
Ulysses S. Grant, nearly five years of fighting had left more than
600,000 Americans dead.

About This Book

This book focuses on the five years of the conflict, from 1861
to 1865. It contains two different types of timelines. Along the
bottom of the pages is a timeline that covers the whole period.
It lists key events and developments, color coded. Each chapter
also has its own timeline, running vertically down the sides of
the pages. This timeline provides more specific details about the
particular subject of the chapter.

Soldiers in the war were often very young, like this Confederate private. In many cases, sons fought alongside their fathers. ↓

Causes of the Conflict

To both the North and the South, the Civil War was justified as self-defense: defense of the Union for the North and defense of Southern freedoms for the South.

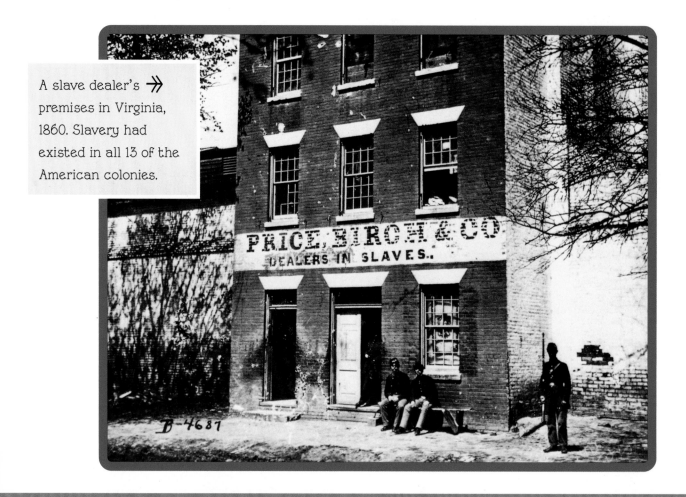

A slave dealer's → premises in Virginia, 1860. Slavery had existed in all 13 of the American colonies.

Timeline
1861 January–March

January 2 South Carolina
Confederate troops occupy Fort Johnson in Charleston Harbor.

January 11 Alabama
Alabama is the fourth state to leave the Union.

January 26 Louisiana
Louisiana is the sixth state to leave the Union.

January

February

January 9 Mississippi
Mississippi becomes the second state to join the Confederacy.

January 10 Florida
Florida leaves the Union.

January 19 Georgia
Georgia leaves the Union.

KEY:

Politics

Land war

Sea war

At the heart of the quarrel was black slavery. Slavery had existed in the Americas since the earliest days of the 17th century, when slave labor was a key feature of the Southern plantation system. Colonists grew crops such as tobacco, sugar, rice, and cotton that required many workers, which the slave trade provided cheaply.

At independence, there were about 600,000 slaves in the new country. Almost all of them were in the South. In many northern states, slavery became illegal. In the South, meanwhile, cotton plantations came to dominate the economy—and they relied on slavery.

Expansion of the Country

The rapid growth of the United States in the first half of the 19th century brought the question of slavery to the fore. As new territories were admitted to the Union, would they be slave or free states?

In 1819, Missouri applied to join the Union as a slave state. Many northerners objected, but Missouri's wish was granted. As a balance, Maine became a free state. In the so-called Missouri Compromise, slavery was forbidden north of latitude 36° 30'.

Timeline

1787 Northwest Ordinance outlaws slavery northwest of the Ohio River.

1803 The Lousiana Purchase—of French-owned land—doubles the size of the nation.

1820 Missouri Compromise: Missouri enters the Union as slave state.

1846–1848 Mexican War adds territory in the West and Southwest.

1854 Kansas–Nebraska Act creates two new territories, with the settlers entitled to decide on the issue of slavery.

1860 Election of Abraham Lincoln as president brings slavery issue to a head.

← When they arrived in the United States, slaves were kept in cramped cells while they waited to be sold.

February 4 Alabama
Southern leaders write a new constitution for the Confederate States of America. Jefferson Davis is chosen as president.

March 4 Washington, DC Abraham Lincoln is inaugurated as 16th president of the United States; he announces "I have no purpose, directly or indirectly, to interfere with the institution of slavery in the States where it exists."

March

February 7 Alabama/ Mississippi
The Choctaw Indian Nation makes an alliance with the Southern states; other native peoples follow in 1861.

February 26 Alabama
The Confederate Congress establishes a general staff for the Army of the Confederate States.

March 11 Alabama
The Confederate Congress adopts the Constitution of the Confederate States of America.

Dred Scott

In 1846, the Missouri slave Dred Scott sued for his freedom on the grounds that he had lived for many years in a free state. The Supreme Court finally decreed in 1857 that Scott was still a slave, blacks were not citizens of the United States, and that laws banning slavery in parts of the US were illegal. The ruling appalled many people in the North.

The Abolition Movement

The slavery debate grew more bitter. In the North, abolitionists were a small but powerful minority. Southerners believed they threatened the whole basis of southern life. In 1852, Harriet Beecher Stowe's novel *Uncle Tom's Cabin* intensified the debate with its powerful exposure of the cruel conditions of slavery.

A further compromise, the Kansas-Nebraska Act of 1854, allowed people in those territories to decide for themselves whether to be free or slave states. Abolitionists and slavers came to blows over the future of "Bleeding Kansas." Meanwhile, the Dred Scott case of 1857 (see box, left) and John Brown's failed attempt to start a slave uprising in 1859 encouraged abolitionist sympathy in the North.

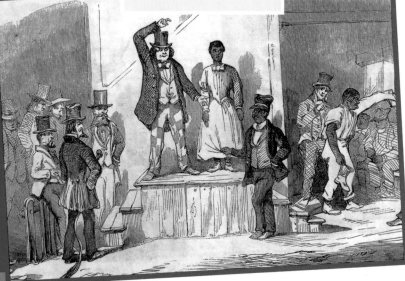

A female slave is sold at auction. Families were often sold separately and split up forever. ⇓

A New President

The election of Abraham Lincoln of the new Republican Party as president in

Timeline

1861 April–June

KEY:

Politics

Land war

Sea war

April   May

April 12 South Carolina
Confederate troops attack Fort Sumter in Charleston Harbor.

April 15 Washington, DC
President Lincoln calls for the Northern states to raise an army of 75,000 troops to fight the South.

April 13 South Carolina
Fort Sumter surrenders to the Confederates. The Civil War has begun.

April 19 Washington, DC
Lincoln orders a naval blockade of the Southern states.

April 23 Virginia Major General Robert E. Lee becomes commander of land and naval forces in Virginia.

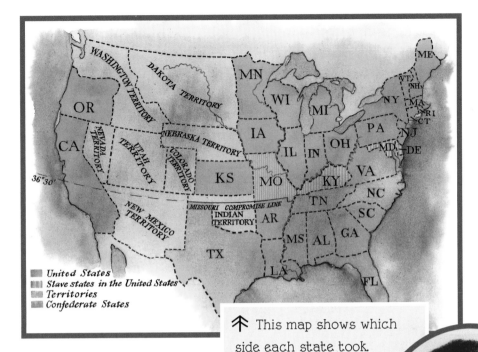

United States
Slave states in the United States
Territories
Confederate States

↑ This map shows which side each state took. Four slave states chose to remain in the Union.

November 1860 dismayed the South. Lincoln and the Republicans—who drew all their support from the North and the West—had campaigned strongly against any extension of slavery. To accept the new president was, to most Southerners, to accept second-class status in the Union. To them, secession—leaving the Union— seemed the only answer.

John Brown

John Brown saw slavery as a sin against God. In October 1859, he led a raid on the federal arsenal at Harpers Ferry in Virginia, hoping to start a slave uprising. He was caught and hanged for murder. His bearing at his trial gained him sympathy in the North. More Southerners concluded that it was time to leave the Union.

« John Brown was a passionate idealist motivated by his religious beliefs.

May 9 Britain Great Britain announces its intention to remain neutral during the war.

June 10 Virginia West Virginia breaks from Virginia and the Confederacy, and joins the Union as a separate state.

June

May 20 North Carolina North Carolina becomes the last state to leave the Union.

June 10 Virginia In one of the first battles of the war, 1,200 Confederates defeat 3,500 Union troops at Big Bethel.

Secession and First Shots

Between December 1860 and June 1861, 11 Southern states seceded from, or left, the Union. They believed they had the right to leave if the federal government abused its power.

In this engraving, ➤ Confederates bombard Fort Sumter from the shores of Charleston Harbor on April 13, 1861.

Timeline
1861
July–
September

July 21 Virginia The First Battle of Manassas, also called First Bull Run, is the first major battle of Civil War. The Confederates resist a determined Union attack, and Union troops retreat in panic toward Washington, DC.

August 10 Missouri The Battle of Wilson's Creek is the first battle west of the Mississippi River; the Confederates win an encounter that leaves 2,500 casualties.

July

August

July 2 Wisconsin Union forces push back Confederates in the Battle of Hoke's Run.

August 26 West Virginia Confederates force Union troops to retreat at Kessler's Cross Lanes.

KEY:

 Politics

Land war

Sea war

The emergence of the Republican Party in the North in the latter 1850s pushed moderate Southerners to consider secession. Republicans would keep slavery out of new territories in the West, which secessionists believed would lead to the abolition of slavery. As the 1860 election drew near, they argued that the election of the Republican candidate, Abraham Lincoln, would justify secession.

A Northern cartoon attacks the seceding states for pulling apart the Union, shown as a cow.

The Upper South Holds Back

Only the seven states of the Deep South had viewed Lincoln's election as sufficient cause for secession. The slave states of the upper South generally shared the proslavery views of the seceding Deep South states, but they knew that if war came, much of the fighting would take place on their soil. Slavery was not as

Timeline

November 6, 1860
Abraham Lincoln is elected president.

December 17, 1860
South Carolina votes to leave the Union.

January 1861
Alabama, Florida, Georgia, Louisiana, and Mississippi secede.

February 1861
Texas secedes. The Confederate States of America is created.

March 4, 1861 Lincoln is sworn in as president.

April 12, 1861 First shots of the Civil War are fired as Confederate troops attack Union-controlled Fort Sumter.

April 17, 1861 Virginia secedes from the Union.

May 20, 1861 North Carolina becomes the last state to leave the Union.

September 12–15 West Virginia In the Battle of Cheat Mountain Summit, Robert E. Lee, future hero of the Confederacy, is defeated despite having stronger forces than the enemy.

September 17 Missouri The Confederate campaign in Missouri continues with another victory, in the Battle of Liberty.

September

August 28–29 North Carolina Union troops capture shore batteries around Hatteras Inlet in an amphibious raid.

September 13 Missouri Confederates begin a week-long battle that forces the surrender of Union troops in Lexington.

September 19 Kentucky A large Confederate force raids the Union guerrilla training base in Barbourville, but finds the camp largely empty.

Pierre G.T. Beauregard

General Pierre Gustave Toussaint Beauregard became a popular Confederate hero for his role at Fort Sumter. Born into a Creole family in Louisiana, he graduated from West Point. After Louisiana left the Union in 1861, Beauregard resigned from the US Army. After Fort Sumter, he took command of the Confederate army in northern Virginia. He saw action in every major theater of the war, making general after the First Battle of Bull Run.

important to the economies of Maryland, Delaware, Kentucky, and Missouri as it was to the Deep South cotton-producing states.

Lincoln's Response

Lincoln's inaugural address (opening speech) repeated his intention not to interfere with slavery where it already existed. But he issued a warning to the seceded states, promising that the federal government would "hold, occupy, and possess" forts and other properties that were still under Union control in the South. This soon focused attention on Fort Sumter, a federal fort on an island in Charleston Harbor in South Carolina.

↑ An excellent engineer, P. G. T. Beauregard was one of eight full generals to join the Confederate army.

Confederate Dilemma

Confederate president Jefferson Davis realized the Union could not keep a garrison on Confederate soil without compromising Confederate

Timeline
1861
October–December

October 21 Missouri Battle of Fredericktown. Union troops push back Confederates to win control of southeastern Missouri.

November 7 Missouri Ulysses S. Grant, future commander of all Union armies, defeats Confederate forces at Belmont near the Mississippi River, but withdraws after a counterattack.

October

November

KEY:

Politics

Land war

Sea war

October 21 Kentucky Some 7,000 Union troops defeat Confederates in the Battle of Camp Wildcat.

October 21 Virginia In the Battle of Ball's Bluff, Union forces fail to cross the Potomac River at Harrison's Island to attack Leesburg.

November 8 Kentucky In the Battle of Ivy Mountain, a large Union force fights off an ambush and pushes the enemy back into Virginia.

independence. If he did not act, others in the South might. He ordered General Pierre G. T. Beauregard to take the fort before the Union could send reinforcements. On April 12, 1861, Confederate guns opened fire, and two days later the fort surrendered without loss of life.

More Secession

The next day, Lincoln called up 75,000 state militia, signaling his intention to fight. This set in motion a second wave of secession, including Virginia. Virginia was crucial to the South. It was the most populous Southern state, it was located in a critical position across the Potomac River from Washington, DC, and it had the greatest industrial capacity of any Southern state. Meanwhile, four slave states—Delaware, Kentucky, Maryland, and Missouri—never did leave the Union.

↓ An engraving depicts a crowded secession meeting in Charleston, South Carolina. South Carolina was the first state to secede from the Union.

November 19 Oklahoma
Confederate troops attack and defeat Unionist Creek and Seminole Indians at the Battle of Round Mountain.

December 21 At the Battle of Dranesville, Union troops defeat "Jeb" Stuart's Confederate cavalry in northern Virginia.

December

November 8 Cuba A diplomatic incident begins when Union sailors illegally seize Confederate officials from a British ship; the Union apologizes after British protests.

December 9 Oklahoma Confederates continue to harass retreating Creek and Seminole at the Battle of Chusto-Talasah.

The First Battle of Bull Run

Also called the First Battle of Manassas, the First Battle of Bull Run was the first of many large-scale encounters between the Union and Confederate armies.

Similarities in the ⟶ uniforms and flags of the two sides added to the confusion of the battle.

Timeline
1862 January– March

January 3 Virginia Union gunboats bombard Confederate coastal batteries guarding the Potomac at Cockpit Point.

January 10 Kentucky At the Battle of Middle Creek, Union troops halt the Confederates' 1861 offensive in Kentucky.

January   February

KEY:

Politics

Land war

Sea war

January 5–6 Maryland Confederate general "Stonewall" Jackson fails to force the surrender of the town of Hancock.

January 18 Arizona The Confederate Territory of Arizona is created from part of New Mexico.

January 19 Kentucky Union counterattacks push the Confederates back from Logan's Crossroads to Murfreesboro, Tennessee.

A view of Bull Run Creek showing an army pontoon bridge and Union troops.

In July 1861, both sides were sure that the war would be short and relatively bloodless, and that one grand campaign would decide the war in their favor. The First Battle of Bull Run showed both sides that the war would be long and bloody.

Battle Preparations

By early summer, Lincoln faced huge popular pressure to send his large army of volunteers to march on the new Confederate capital at Richmond, Virginia.

Timeline

July 16 McDowell's Union troops head toward Manassas.

July 18 The Confederates use Manassas Gap Railroad to reinforce Beauregard's troops.

July 18 Union troops try to cross Bull Run Creek.

July 21, morning Union troops cross Bull Run Creek.

July 21, late morning Confederates pushed back to Henry Hill.

July 21, afternoon Fighting continues on Henry Hill. Two Confederate armies unite just as Confederates appear to be losing. Jackson attacks.

July 21, late afternoon Exhausted Union troops begin to retreat.

July 21, evening Union retreat descends into chaos as Confederates shell road to Washington.

February 6 Tennessee Union general Ulysses S. Grant captures Confederate Fort Henry. The Union now controls the Tennessee River as far south as Alabama.

March 8 Virginia The Battle of Hampton Roads. The Confederate ironclad CSS *Virginia* sinks two Union wooden ships and damages another.

March 17 Virginia Union troops ship to the tip of the Virginia "peninsula," marking the start of the Peninsular Campaign.

March

February 16 Tennessee Union troops under Grant capture Fort Donelson and take around 15,000 Southern prisoners.

February 25 Tennessee Nashville becomes the first Confederate capital to fall to Union troops.

March 9 Virginia CSS *Virginia* returns to Hampton Roads but is met by the Union ironclad USS *Monitor*. A four-hour, close-range battle ends in stalemate.

Battle Details

1. On July 18, a Union detachment tried to cross Bull Run Creek. It was pushed back in a skirmish that lasted all afternoon.

2. On July 21, the main Union force made a flanking movement, crossing Bull Run Creek at Sudley Ford at 9:30 A.M. After fighting on Matthew's Hill, the Confederates fell back to Henry Hill by late morning.

3. Fighting continued on Henry Hill. After reinforcements arrived, Thomas "Stonewall" Jackson led a Confederate counterattack. By late afternoon, Union troops were in retreat.

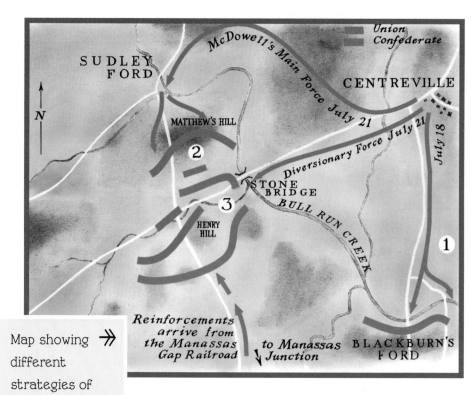

Map showing different strategies of the two armies.

General Irvin McDowell protested that his army of citizen-soldiers was not ready, but public demand was irresistible, and he was ordered to set out for Richmond in early July.

McDowell's target was the equally inexperienced Confederate army, commanded by Pierre G. T. Beauregard, McDowell's classmate at West Point. His army was stationed just north of Manassas Junction close to Washington, on Bull Run Creek. Manassas was a key Confederate supply depot and railroad stop.

Timeline
1862 April–June

April 6 Tennessee Heavy fighting at the Battle of Shiloh. Confederate troops outnumber the Union troops, but halt their attack because of exhaustion.

April 12 Georgia In the "Great Locomotive Chase," Union agents steal a Confederate train, but are chased, caught, and executed.

April

May

April 7 Tennessee Fighting continues at the Battle of Shiloh with huge losses on both sides. Confederates lose ground gained previous day, and the battle ends with no gain on either side.

April 29 Louisiana The Union captures New Orleans, opening the Mississippi valley to invasion.

KEY:

Politics

Land war

Sea war

The Napoleon gun was used by both sides. It was a smoothbore weapon with a range of 1,600 yards (1,460 m). →

"Stonewall" Jackson

Thomas J. Jackson was a West Point graduate who joined the Confederacy out of loyalty to his home state, Virginia. His nickname came from his stand at Bull Run, which also saw him promoted to major general. His accidental death in 1863, when he was shot by his own men, was a huge blow to the Confederate cause.

Main Battle

McDowell attacked first. His army pushed the Confederates back to Henry Hill. By the afternoon, the Confederates were almost defeated, but then reinforcements arrived. Commander Thomas J. Jackson led a counterattack that earned his nickname of "Stonewall." By evening, the Union army was beaten.

First Bull Run was small compared to later battles (1,900 Confederate and 2,800 Union casualties), but it was the initial exposure to combat for many of the war's commanders, and it had proved the importance of railroads in troop movements. It also dispelled all illusions of a quick resolution to the war.

← "Stonewall" Jackson became a hero because of his battle tactics and speed.

May 25 Virginia A Confederate victory at Winchester relieves pressure on Richmond.

May 31 Virginia The Battle of the Seven Pines is drawn, with heavy losses on both sides.

June 12 Virginia "Jeb" Stuart leads 1,200 Confederate cavalry on a three-day ride to seize 165 Union men on the Virginia Peninsula outside Richmond, Virginia.

June

May 15 Virginia Five Union gunboats advance up the James River toward Richmond, but are forced back by Confederate gunfire.

June 6 Tennessee Union ships launch an attack on Memphis and capture the city after a short battle.

June 25 Virginia At Oak Grove near Richmond, Confederates launch a counterattack that is the first of the Seven Days' Battles.

River War

The South had thousands of miles of rivers, and control of them was to be the key to Union victory. The Union navy fought for supremacy over these vital river links.

Riverboats moored at → White House Landing, a key Union supply base during the 1862 Peninsular Campaign.

Timeline
1862
July–
September

July 11 Washington, DC
General Henry Halleck replaces General George B. McClellan as commander of the Union army.

July 13 Washington, DC Lincoln drafts the Emancipation Proclamation, freeing the slaves in the South.

July

August

KEY:

Politics

Land war

Sea war

July 1 Washington, DC
The Union government introduces income tax to help pay for the war.

July 17 Washington, DC
The Union government opens the way for the formation of black units in the Union army.

August 14 Virginia The Army of the Potomac begins to withdraw from Harrison's Landing, ending the Peninsular Campaign.

The Union navy had a growing fleet of wooden sailing ships and steamships, plus new ironclad gunboats. It could thus overwhelm Confederate river defenses, preventing the South from using its rivers for transportation. Once the rivers were secured, the Union could use them to move troops and supplies through Tennessee, Mississippi, and Louisiana. The Confederate navy, suffering from shortages of men and materials, could not match its Union opponents.

River War in the West

The river war in the West occurred roughly in three phases. During the first, from January to March

The Union river gunboat USS *Fort Hindman* patrolled the Mississippi River. ⇓

Timeline

February 6, 1862 Union gunboats capture Fort Henry after a bombardment.

February 16, 1862 Union troops capture Fort Donelson with help from gunboats. The Tennessee and the Cumberland Rivers are now in Union hands as far as Corinth, Mississippi, and Florence, Alabama.

March 9, 1862 The drawn naval battle between ironclads CSS *Virginia* and USS *Monitor* at Hampton Roads leads to acceleration in ironclad shipbuilding program.

April 16–28, 1862 Union naval victory takes Fort Jackson and St. Philip on the Mississippi.

July 4, 1863 Last Confederate fort on the Mississippi surrenders; Union naval forces now control the whole river.

1864 Red River Expedition ends in failure for Union troops trying to move up Red River and find way into Texas.

August 29 Virginia The Second Battle of Manassas (Second Bull Run) lasts two days and ends in a Confederate victory that defeats a Union attempt to capture Richmond.

September 24, Tennessee In revenge for Confederate shelling of his gunboats, Union general William Sherman orders the destruction of every house in the town of Randolph.

September

September 17 Maryland The Battle of Antietam ends in a draw after Confederates resist a Union attack at the Bloody Lane for four hours. Both sides suffer large casualties.

September 18 Missouri Ten Confederate prisoners are executed in what is known as the Massacre at Palmyra.

September 22 Washington, DC Lincoln issues the Emancipation Proclamation. It will take effect on January 1, 1863.

Battle of Shiloh

The battle fought on April 6–7, 1862, began when Confederate general Albert S. Johnston's army surprised a Union army at Shiloh Church, Tennessee. Some of the fiercest fighting of the war took place in a peach orchard. The buzzing noise of bullets gave it the name "the Hornet's Nest." The battle cost the South 10,700 killed and wounded for no gain, while the North narrowly avoided defeat at a cost of 13,000 casualties.

1862, Union forces concentrated on the Tennessee and the Cumberland Rivers. The campaign included one of the war's bloodiest encounters at Shiloh Church, near Pittsburg Landing on the Tennessee. In a two-day battle, nearly 24,000 soldiers were killed or wounded for little gain on either side.

The second phase of the river war, between March 1862 and July 1863, saw the Union try to gain control of the Mississippi River.

The least successful of the three phases of the river war came from March to May 1864 on the Red River, when Union troops were almost stranded at Alexandria, Louisana, when the river's water levels fell.

↑ River transportation was invaluable for moving Union troops to war theaters in the South.

River War in the East

In the east, the York and the James Rivers were crucial in the 1862 Peninsular Campaign. In March 1862, Union general George B. McClellan moved his army via

Timeline
1862 October–December

October 3–4 Mississippi Union forces in the city of Corinth resist an attack by 22,000 Confederates.

October 8 Kentucky Union victory in the Battle of Perryville forces the Confederates to retreat from Kentucky into eastern Tennessee.

October

November

KEY:

Politics

Land war

Sea war

October 4 Texas After a Union blockade, the port of Galveston is forced to surrender.

November 7 Washington, DC Abraham Lincoln appoints Ambrose E. Burnside as commander of the Army of the Potomac to replace George B. McClellan, whom Lincoln thinks is not aggressive enough.

↑ An engraving of the Battle of Shiloh depicts Union troops fighting to recapture artillery.

Battle Details

1. Johnston's Confederates make a surprise attack early on April 6. Johnston is killed; Beauregard takes command.
2. Confederates push back Union troops to the river.
3. Grant's Union army is reinforced during the night.
4. Union troops counterattack on April 7 and make progress. In the late afternoon, Beauregard orders his men to withdraw.

Chesapeake Bay to Fortress Monroe, Virginia. He used river transports to establish a supply depot at White House Landing, only 20 miles (32 km) from Richmond.

Natural Defenses

Rivers were a major obstacle for Union armies in Virginia. Most of the rivers run west to east through the state, while Union troops generally advanced north to south (apart from the Peninsular Campaign). They formed a natural line of defense for the Confederate army.

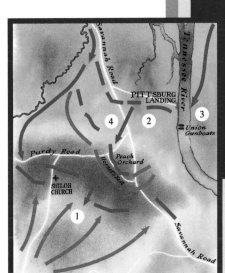

← This map shows the main stages (see box above) of the Battle of Shiloh.

December 13 Virginia Eager to prove himself, Burnside tries to cross the Rappahannock River and advance on Richmond. In the Battle of Fredericksburg, he loses 6,500 men in 14 failed attacks on Confederate lines.

December 31 Tennessee Union troops eventually prevail at the Battle of Murfreesboro after being initially forced to fall back.

December

December 7 Tennessee The Battle of Hartsville. A Confederate attack defeats Union troops guarding the Cumberland River, opening the way to western Tennessee and Kentucky.

December 14 Virginia The Battle of Fredericksburg. Burnside is persuaded by his officers not to launch more attacks. It is a great Confederate victory.

Home Front

For Southern civilians, the effects of the war were more immediate than for Northerners. Their lives changed totally while life in the North was largely unaffected.

A Northern engraving ⇒ shows Southern women urging their men to go to war, then suffering the consequences later.

Timeline
1863
January–
March

January 1 Washington, DC
The Emancipation Proclamation comes into effect. The Civil War becomes a struggle to free the slaves as well as to preserve the Union.

January 29 Idaho Union soldiers seeking revenge on Native American allies of the Confederates kill over 380 Shoshoni at the Boa Ogoi camp.

January

February

KEY:

Politics

Land war

Sea war

January 20–22 Virginia The Union Army of the Potomac advances toward Lee, but rain softens the ground and the "Mud March" is bogged down.

January 30–31 South Carolina
Two Confederate ironclads break the Union blockade of Charleston.

Most Southerners welcomed the war, and men enlisted enthusiastically. With three out of four eligible men serving in the Confederate army, the Southern home front was largely a world of women, children, and slaves. Women often had to take charge of family farms when the men were away fighting. On some plantations, owners' wives took over day-to-day affairs. Many found managing their slaves the most challenging aspect of their new duties.

Twenty Slave Law

Early in the war, a new law exempted white men from military service if they ran plantations with more than 20 slaves. Poorer families who had no slaves or whose women were forced to labor in the fields when their husbands were away resented this favoring of the upper classes.

Timeline

1860 On the eve of war, the North is home to 21.6 million whites, 248,000 free blacks, and 430,000 slaves; the South has 5.4 million whites, 133,000 free blacks, and 3.5 million slaves.

1862 Confederate draft is introduced. Southerners suffer from severe food shortages, while the Union economy continues to prosper.

1863, March Union draft introduced.

1863, July Antidraft riots in Northern cities.

1864 Ulysses S. Grant's plan to "squeeze the South" creates 250,000 refugees.

← Students at the Academy of Fine Arts in Philadelphia making a flag. Such civilian activities helped keep up morale.

February 3 Tenneessee Having failed in a mission to disupt shipping on the Cumberland River, Confederate cavalry make an unsuccessful and bloody attack on the Union garrison at Dover.

March 6 Virginia The unpopular Confederate impressment law gives officers the right to take food from farmers at fixed prices.

March

March 3 Washington, DC The Union government introduces the National Conscription Act, which is deeply unpopular with those forced into military service.

March 8 Maryland Confederate guerrilla leader John Mosby leads a raid behind enemy lines to Fairfax Court House, taking Union prisoners and horses before returning to Confederate lines.

Bread Riots

By spring 1863, stores of grain in the South were running out. Prices rose rapidly. People accused stores and the government of hoarding supplies. In some places, "bread riots" broke out. The worst was in Richmond, Virginia. Several hundred women smashed store windows and seized food and goods. Confederate president Jefferson Davis came to calm the rioters. Despite his appeals, they refused to leave until he threatened to order the militia to open fire, when they dispersed.

This is an example ↑ of the classical Greek Revival style of plantation homes built before the war.

Shortages and Refugees

By 1862, food shortages in the South were severe. This was partly the effect of the Union blockade and partly the result of a poor distribution system that prioritized military supplies. There were shortages of salt—for preserving meat—iron for railroad tracks, coffee, and manufactured cloth. Prices rose sevenfold, so many people could no longer afford even basic foods.

In addition, as many as 250,000 Southerners became refugees as Union armies invaded the South. Rural families whose homes and farms lay in the path of the invading troops fled to cities such as Richmond, Columbia, and Atlanta, which became overcrowded and chaotic as a result.

Timeline
1863
April– June

April 2 Virginia "Bread riots" break out in the Confederacy because of high food prices.

May 3 Virginia The Battle of Chancellorsville. A renewed Confederate attack pushes back Union forces.

April

May

KEY:

Politics

Land war

Sea war

April 17 Mississippi Union cavalry raid Mississippi, tearing up railroad lines before heading south to Baton Rouge, Louisiana.

May 2 Virginia During the Confederate victory at the Battle of Chancellorsville, "Stonewall" Jackson is killed by one of his own men.

The North

The Union home front fared well by comparison. The North had a far larger industrial base, and people on the home front had a key role in keeping the economy buoyant. Many men enlisted, but enough remained to manage farms or work in industries. They were joined by a growing number of women, mainly as unskilled laborers. Women also entered certain kinds of work from which they had been barred. It was almost unheard of for women to work as government clerks or as nurses, for example, but during the war it became commonplace.

← A slave family in Hampton, Virginia, in 1861. Their daily life was strictly regulated.

Civilian Fund-Raising

Many Northern cities held fairs to raise funds to provide medical supplies for wounded soldiers and other types of relief. The first was held in Chicago on October 27, 1863. It ran for two weeks and drew 5,000 visitors. President Lincoln donated the original draft of the Emancipation Proclamation, which was the fair's main attraction and sold at auction for $3,000.

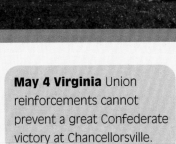

This house was a hospital after the Battle of White Oak Swamp in June 1862. ↓

May 4 Virginia Union reinforcements cannot prevent a great Confederate victory at Chancellorsville.

May 18 Mississippi Grant's Union troops begin the siege of Vicksburg.

June 9 Virginia After a battle of massed cavalry charges, Confederates eventually gain victory at the Battle of Brandy Station.

June

May 14 Mississippi Union troops capture Jackson, the state capital, and destroy its factories and railroads.

June 14 Virginia Victory in the Battle of Winchester allows Robert E. Lee's Army of Northern Virginia to invade the North with 75,000 men.

June 16 Robert E. Lee's army crosses the Potomac River, intending to win a decisive victory in Pennsylvania and capture Washington, DC. Southern morale is high.

Emancipation Proclamation

On January 1, 1863, Lincoln's Emancipation Proclamation
came into effect. It declared "all persons held as slaves
within a State" were "thenceforward, and forever free."

African Americans →
wait up for New Year's
Day 1863, when the new
law comes into effect.

Timeline
1863
July–
September

July 1 Pennsylvania The largest battle
of the Civil War, Gettysburg, ranges
75,000 Confederates agains 90,000 Union
soldiers of the Army of the Potomac.

July 3 Pennsylvania At Gettysburg, an attack by 15,000
Confederates—Pickett's Charge—fails, marking the
effective end of the battle. Some 6,000 men are dead.
The Confederate failure is the turning point of the war.

July   August

KEY:

Politics

Land war

Sea war

July 2 Pennsylvania
During a day of fierce fighting
at Gettysburg, Union troops
halt Confederate attacks.

July 4 Mississippi Vicksburg
surrenders, splitting the
Confederacy in two.

July 13 New York
Antidraft riots break out
across the North,
including in New York City.

Lincoln's decree ensured that the Civil War became a war of black liberation as well as a struggle to save the Union. Lincoln had often said that his responsibility as president was to suppress the South's rebellion, not to free its slaves. But slavery lay at the very heart of the conflict and had to be addressed. By late 1862, Lincoln judged there was enough public support to incorporate slave emancipation into his policy.

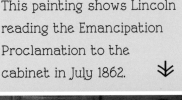

This painting shows Lincoln reading the Emancipation Proclamation to the cabinet in July 1862.

Timeline

1861 Union Army turns away free black volunteers.

September 17, 1862 Union victory at Antietam gives Lincoln a position of strength to tackle the slavery controversy.

September 22, 1862 The Emancipation Proclamation gives rebellious states an ultimatum to rejoin the Union or all existing slaves will be declared free.

January 1, 1863 The final Emancipation Proclamation is issued.

Spring 1863 Free blacks and former slaves rush to join Union army.

March 3, 1865 The Freedmen's Bureau is set up.

December 18, 1865 Thirteenth Amendment to the Constitution finally abolishes slavery.

September 6–8 South Carolina A Union marine and infantry assault at Charleston Harbor wins Fort Wagner but not Fort Sumter.

September 20 Tennessee The Battle of Chickamauga ends with Confederate victory; Union forces retreat to Chattanooga, but with 18,000 casualties, the Confederates cannot push home the advantage.

September

August 20 Kansas Confederate guerrillas led by William Quantrill attack the antislavery town of Lawrence, killing 150 male civilians.

September 19 Tennessee In the Battle of Chickamauga, 65,000 Confederates face 62,000 Union soldiers.

Abraham Lincoln

No other American leader (except perhaps George Washington) had such an impact on the nation's development as Lincoln, particularly his freeing of the slaves. His eloquent speeches also gave meaning to the Civil War for future generations. With his actions and words, the 16th president gave the nation "a new birth of freedom."

An illustrated ➤ print of Lincoln's Emancipation Proclamation.

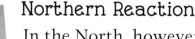

Southern Reaction

The South reacted furiously to the decree that slaves under Southern control were free. President Jefferson Davis called it an "effort to excite servile war within the Confederacy." Davis warned that "all negro slaves captured in arms"—meaning many black soldiers serving in Union armies—would be tried under Confederate slave laws.

A slave reads news ⤊ of the proclamation.

Northern Reaction

In the North, however, abolitionists, African Americans, and others welcomed the emancipation. Leading abolitionist Frederick Douglass congratulated Lincoln on "this amazing approximation toward the sacred truth of human liberty." Many others pointed out, however, that the proclamation was very limited, freeing

Timeline
1863 October– December

October 5 South Carolina
The CSS *David* damages the USS *New Ironsides* in Charleston Harbor with a spar torpedo.

October 15 South Carolina The *H.L. Hunley*, an experimental Confederate submarine, sinks during a training exercise, killing seven of its crew of nine.

October

November

October 14 Virginia At the Battle of Bristoe Station, an error by Confederate general A. P. Hill leads his men into a Union ambush.

November 19 Pennsylvania At the dedication of a battlefield cemetery, Abraham Lincoln delivers the Gettysburg Address: he promises that "government of the people, by the people, for the people, shall not perish from the earth."

KEY:

 Politics

 Land war

 Sea war

slaves only in areas still under Confederate control—not in the loyal border states or in Union-controlled parts of the Confederacy.

Effect of the Proclamation

Despite its limitations, the proclamation began the process of freeing the South's slaves. It did not end slavery—that came with the Thirteenth Amendment in December 1865—but it gave the Union cause a moral force and strengthened it both militarily and politically. It also ended any chance of foreign intervention: no European country was prepared to oppose a crusade against slavery. As for African Americans themselves, they still had many more battles to fight before they would become truly free.

African American children attend school in a freedmen's village ⇓ in Arlington, Virginia.

Freedmen's Bureau

Established in March 1865, the Freedmen's Bureau was one of the first federal social service agencies. It was intended to help with every aspect of life for refugees (both black and white), and newly freed slaves in the South. Its major success was in providing education for freed children and adults, for many of whom it was a first chance to go to school. All today's major black colleges were founded or helped by the bureau. It closed in 1872 after only seven years of operation.

November 24–25 Tennessee
Union forces at Chattanooga storm Cemetery Ridge to secure the city and its vital food supplies.

December 14–15 Tennessee The Battle of Bean's Station ends in a Confederate victory over 4,000 Union soldiers.

December

November 23 Tennessee
Battle of Chattanooga begins when Union troops push back the Confederate siege.

December 9 Tennessee A 17-day siege of Union troops in Knoxville ends when Confederate forces withdraw after Union reinforcements arrive.

December 29 Tennessee
Cavalry fighting at Mossy Creek sees rebel forces pushed back and the Union in control of the area.

The Battle of Gettysburg

Over three days, the largest battle of the Civil War was fought between Lee's Confederate army and Meade's Union army at Gettysburg, Pennsylvania, in July 1863.

Confederate Louisiana ➔➔ Tigers advance on a Union battery on the second day of Gettysburg, July 2, 1863.

Timeline
1864
January–March

January 17 Tennessee The Battle of Dandridge is a Confederate victory but does not seriously harm Union forces.

January 27 Tennessee A Confederate incursion against Union forces near Dandridge is halted at the Battle of Fair Garden.

January

February

KEY:

Politics

Land war

Sea war

January 26 Alabama After a two-hour assault, Confederate cavalry fail to capture Athens, despite their superior numbers.

February 14 Mississippi Major General William T. Sherman begins a week-long raid that destroys a key railroad junction at Meridian.

The encounter began almost by chance when foraging Confederate soldiers ran into Union cavalry west of Gettysburg. The town was always a potential battleground. It was strategically important because it lay at the junction of roads that led to Washington, Baltimore, and Harrisburg, the capital of Pennsylvania. Generals Robert E. Lee and George G. Meade quickly ordered their respective Confederate and Union commanders to concentrate their forces on the town.

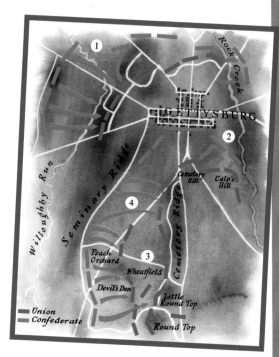

Battle Details

July 1, 1863 Confederates advance from the north (1) and occupy Gettysburg. Union forces retreat to high ground south of the town.

July 2, 1863 Union forces pushed back as fierce fighting takes place at Devil's Den and Peach Orchard, but Union line holds (3).

July 2, late afternoon Piecemeal Confederate attacks on Cemetery Hill and Culp's Hill make no headway (2).

July 3, 1863 15,000 Confederate troops make doomed frontal assault, later called Pickett's Charge. The failure of the attack marks the end of the battle (4).

July 4, 1863 Lee orders defeated troops back to Virginia.

← Confederate troops advance at Gettysburg on July 3, 1863, in the attack known as Pickett's Charge.

February 22 Georgia The Battle of Dalton is an inconclusive clash at Crow Valley, near Dalton.

March 14 Louisiana Union troops enter the Confederate Trans-Mississippi Department and capture Fort DeRussy.

March

February 20 Florida Union forces, including a black regiment, are forced to give up an expedition to disrupt Confederate supply lines near Jacksonville.

March 2 Washington, DC Ulysses S. Grant is made commander of all the armies of the Union.

March 25 Kentucky Confederates assault the city of Paducah on the Ohio River, but withdraw after heavy casualties.

Photography

The Civil War was the first US conflict to be captured by photography. For the first time, graphic images brought the brutality of war to the home front. Pioneers such as Mathew Brady took images that were printed in many newspapers. Although the images only showed the aftermath of battle—cameras were not quick enough to capture action—they profoundly changed how the public saw the war.

The First Day

Union troops advanced from the south, Confederates from the north and northwest. Union forces were pushed back from Gettysburg and were on the verge of losing the battle when they were rallied by the arrival of reinforcements. By nightfall, the Confederates held the town, but Union forces were secure to the south on Cemetery Hill and Culp's Hill.

The Second Day

Both armies reinforced overnight. By July 2, more than 93,000 Union men were in position on the hills and Cemetery Ridge. Fighting began in the afternoon with a disaster for the Union as III Corps, advancing without orders, was destroyed in savage fighting around the Peach Orchard and Devil's Den. However, Union defenses on the high ground held. As night fell, Lee's piecemeal attacks on the Union flanks had made no gains.

Harvest of Death shows slain soldiers in the field after the Battle of Gettysburg. ⇓

Timeline
1864 April–June

April 8 Louisiana A Union advance up the Red River ends when its gunboats are forced to retreat; stranded by falling water levels, the Union force has to build dams to allow the boats to escape.

April 12 Tennessee Confederates massacre the Union garrison at Fort Pillow, including 202 of the 262 black troops. "Remember Fort Pillow" becomes a rallying cry among black troops.

April

May

April 9 Louisiana Union troops retreating from Red River face a major Confederate attack at the Battle of Pleasant Hill.

May 3 Virginia Grant moves the Army of the Potomac south to meet Lee's army, but his men have to cross the marshy Wilderness.

May 5 The Battle of the Wilderness. Lee's and Grant's armies fight all day in thick undergrowth.

KEY:

Politics

Land war

Sea war

The Gettysburg Address

Lincoln's speech in November 1863 at the dedication of a new war cemetery at Gettysburg was one of the most famous in US history. He explained his view of the war as a larger struggle for democracy and equality. He insisted "…we here highly resolve that these dead shall not have died in vain—that this nation, under God, shall have a new birth of freedom—and that government of the people, by the people, for the people, shall not perish from the earth."

⤒ Union artillery on the summit of Little Round Top on the final day of Gettysburg.

The Third Day

On July 3, Lee made a bid to break the Union center on Cemetery Ridge. At 1:00 P.M., some 150 guns began the biggest Confederate artillery bombardment of the war. At about 3:00 P.M., 15,000 troops led by George E. Pickett began Pickett's Charge. As they advanced across a mile (1.6 km) of open ground, the men were fired on by Union artillery; within 200 yards (180 m) of the Union front line, the infantry opened up. Only a few hundred Confederates survived. As he rode out to meet the shattered survivors, Lee admitted, "It's all my fault. It is I who have lost this fight."

On July 4, Lee ordered his army back to Virginia. More than 20,000 Confederates were killed, wounded, or missing; Union casualties were 23,000. The South was never again able to threaten the Northern capital.

May 12 Virginia One of the bloodiest battles of the war is fought at Spotsylvania Court House; after 24 hours of hand-to-hand combat at the "Bloody Angle," the battle is drawn.

June 3 Virginia Only 11 miles (18 km) from Richmond, Union troops begin a major attack on Lee's army at Cold Harbor but suffer 7,000 casualties for no gain at all; Confederate casualties are only 1,500.

June

May 6 Virginia Brush fires halt the Battle of the Wilderness as soldiers rescue the wounded; the battle is a draw.

May 11 Virginia The South suffers a huge blow when famed cavalry leader "Jeb" Stuart is wounded and killed at the Battle of Yellow Tavern.

June 27 Georgia More Union losses at the Battle of Kennesaw Mountain, where Union forces charge the Confederate lines with bayonets.

March to the Sea

In late 1864, Union general William T. Sherman led his troops on a destructive march through Georgia to the sea and then north through the Carolinas.

A group of Sherman's infantry rest outside some farm buildings they have occupied. →

Timeline

1864
July– September

July 22 Georgia In Atlanta, the Confederate defenders make an unsuccessful attempt to break the Union siege.

July

August

KEY:

 Politics

Land war

Sea war

July 11 Washington, DC Concern sweeps the Union capital when Confederate troops reach the city limits.

July 30 Virginia Union troops explode a huge mine beneath Confederate lines at Petersburg, but fail to take advantage.

Sherman's troops ↑ marched 600 miles (960 km) in just five months.

Timeline

September 3, 1864 Sherman captures Atlanta, Georgia.

November 15 Sherman leaves Atlanta with 60,000 men.

December 21 Sherman captures Savannah.

February 1, 1865 Sherman leaves Savannah.

February 17 Sherman captures Columbia, state capital of South Carolina.

March 19–21 Confederates fail to halt Sherman at the Battle of Bentonville.

April 13 Sherman captures Raleigh, state capital of North Carolina.

April 26 Joseph E. Johnston surrenders to Sherman.

Following his capture of Atlanta, Georgia, on September 3, 1864, Union general William T. Sherman planned to march to Savannah, a port on the Atlantic coast 220 miles (352 km) away. The capture of the port would enable Union ships to supply the army. Sherman also believed that the march would damage Confederate morale.

Sherman burned anything of military value in Atlanta—one-third of the city accidentally burned as well—and on November 15, he set out with 60,000 men to march on Savannah.

← The damage left by the march made Sherman unpopular in the South.

August 5 Alabama At the Battle of Mobile Bay, a Union fleet takes two hours to defeat the Confederate ironclad CSS *Tennessee* and capture the port; the South still controls the city of Mobile.

September 16 Virginia. Confederate troops steal beef supply at Coggins Point to feed hungry Southerners.

September

August 31 Georgia Sherman moves south of Atlanta to cut the city's supply lines; the Confederates leave the city the next day.

Eyewitness

Emma LeConte describes Sherman's troops in Columbia, South Carolina: "The drunken devils roamed about setting fire to every house the flames seemed likely to spare.... They would enter houses and in the presence of helpless women and children, pour turpentine on the beds and set them on fire.... The wind blew a fearful gale, wafting the flames from house to house with frightful rapidity. By midnight the whole town was wrapped in one huge blaze."

In this engraving, former slaves follow the Union army in late 1864.

Unopposed March

The Confederates turned back to Tennessee. This left few forces to oppose Sherman. He spread his army along a wide path, which made it easier to gather supplies. As the troops advanced, they wrecked railroads and anything else that might aid the Confederate war effort. In many cases, the foraging was accompanied by theft and vandalism. Thousands of lawless stragglers who followed the army were beyond military control. Even Sherman's veterans voiced doubts about the harsh treatment of civilians. Some of the worst-treated civilians were African American slaves who were liberated by the Union army.

Timeline
1864
October–December

October 19 Virginia At the Battle of Cedar Creek, Jubal Early's Confederates rout two Union corps but are defeated when Union reinforcements bolster the line; the defeat breaks the back of the Confederate army in the Shenandoah Valley.

October

November

KEY:

 Politics

Land war

 Sea war

October 23 Missouri In the war's largest battle west of the Mississippi, the South fails to break the Union hold on Missouri.

Sherman captured Savannah on December 21, 1864. His next aim was to join forces with Ulysses S. Grant in Virginia and defeat Robert E. Lee's army. Sherman determined to march through the Carolinas. He set out on February 1, 1865.

Sherman in the Carolinas

This march faced more Confederate troops, as well as several swampy rivers. Winter rains had turned the roads to mud. Nevertheless, the Union troops surprised the enemy with their rapid advance.

The destruction in South Carolina was worse than in Georgia. South Carolina had been the first state to secede and was seen by many Union soldiers as responsible for the war. The state capital, Columbia, was burned on February 17–18, 1865, although who started the fire remains a matter of controversy.

By early March, Sherman entered North Carolina. The Confederates failed to stop his progress at Bentonville on March 19–21. A few days later, Sherman occupied Raleigh, the state capital. The war was soon over. Johnston surrendered on April 26. The marches through Georgia and the Carolinas had been decisive. They showed how weak the Confederacy had become, while their destructiveness demoralized the population and hastened its defeat.

↑ These scenes from the "March to the Sea" were published in the North in 1864; Sherman's easy advance was as much of a morale boost for the North as it was demoralizing for the South.

November 8 Washington, DC
Abraham Lincoln is reelected, mainly thanks to the popularity of Sherman's capture of Atlanta in September.

December 9 Georgia Sherman's troops begin to surround the Confederate-held city of Savannah.

December

November 25 New York
Confederate agents set fire to buildings in New York City, but fail in their plan to start a general fire.

November 30 Tennessee At the Battle of Franklin, John Bell Hood's Confederates come close to defeating the Union line, but are ultimately unsuccessful.

December 21 Georgia Union troops enter Georgia, marking a triumphant end to the "March to the Sea."

Siege Warfare

The capture of Vicksburg was essential if the Union was to regain control of the Mississippi River. From May 1862 to July 1863, Grant's army besieged the city.

A Union battery ➔ of mortars lined up at the Siege of Yorktown, Virginia, in April 1862.

Timeline
1865
January–
March

January 15 North Carolina Union forces seal off Wilmington, the only major Confederate port still open and the South's last access to the outside world.

January 19 South Carolina Having completed his infamous "March to the Sea," Union General William T. Sherman vows to push through the Carolinas into Virginia and orders troops into South Carolina.

January

February

KEY:

Politics

Land war

Sea war

February 3 Virginia Peace talks are held on board a boat at Hampton Roads, but Lincoln and the Confederate delegates do not reach a diplomatic ending to the war.

Siege warfare was based on tactics developed by European armies over the previous 200 years. It was slow and destructive. First, the enemy position was surrounded. All routes of escape or resupply were cut off, presenting the enemy with a stark choice—surrender or face slow starvation. The next step was to position the siege artillery, of which the most feared was the mortar. Developed specifically for sieges, this short, squat weapon lobbed shells in a high arc to land inside enemy defenses: there was no way to defend against it.

Vicksburg Under Siege

Union general Ulysses S. Grant targeted Vicksburg from December 1862, but was foiled by the city's defensive position, guarded by the Mississippi.

Timeline

April–May 1862 Siege of Yorktown, Virginia. Inconclusive outcome.

April–May 1863 Siege of Suffolk, Virginia. Inconclusive outcome.

May–July 1863 Siege of Vicksburg, Mississippi. Union victory.

May–July 1863 Siege of Port Hudson, Louisiana. Union victory.

August 1864 Siege of Fort Morgan, Mobile Point, Alabama. Union victory.

August 1864 Siege of Fort Gaines, Alabama. Union victory.

April 1865 Siege of Petersburg, Virginia. Union victory.

← The Union army blows a crater in the defenses around Vicksburg in June 1863.

March 2 Virginia Union cavalry capture 1,500 Confederates at Waynesboro, gaining control of the whole Shenandoah valley.

March 4 Washington, DC President Lincoln makes his second inaugural address, ending with the words, "With malice toward none."

March

February 17 South Carolina As Union troops enter Columbia, bales of cotton are set alight. Fire destroys half the city.

March 3 Washington, DC The US Congress establishes the Freedmen's Bureau to deal with problems caused by the sudden freeing of tens of thousands of slaves.

March 13 Virginia Slaves are allowed to become soldiers in the Confederacy as the Congress in Richmond passes a law authorizing the use of black troops.

Siege of Vicksburg

After Grant reached Vicksburg in May 1862, the Union army set up 220 heavy guns to bombard the city day and night. Inside Vicksburg, the civilian population suffered as badly from the shelling as the defending soldiers. Many took refuge in caves dug out of hillsides behind the city. Food ran out by late June. Pemberton was also running out of ammunition. Grant refused any terms except unconditional surrender, which came on July 4, 1863.

↥ Grant launched a two-pronged attack to take Vicksburg into Union control.

It was not until May 1863 that he managed to trap the Confederate army of John C. Pemberton inside the city. Grant fought off a relieving army led by Joseph E. Johnston and besieged the city.

Digging Trenches

Grant's army dug 15 miles (24 km) of trenches to protect them against artillery fire from within the city. A siege could not be won by artillery alone. The besieging infantry dug trenches closer and closer to the enemy's forward defenses in preparation for the opening of a breach through which an assault could be made. The diggers protected themselves behind a sap-roller, a large basket filled with earth.

Using Explosives

Breaches were also made by digging a tunnel, filling it with gunpowder, and blowing it up. The Union army used this method twice, at Vicksburg in June 1863 and 13 months later in July 1864 at the Siege of Petersburg,

Timeline

1865 April– May

April 2 Virginia
Confederates retreat from Petersburg and, on April 3, from their capital at Richmond.

April 14 Washington, DC
Abraham Lincoln is shot by John Wilkes Booth and fatally wounded while at the theater with his wife.

April 26 North Carolina
Joseph E. Johnston surrenders Southern forces in the West.

April

April 9 Virginia Surrounded and outnumbered, General Robert E. Lee surrenders to General Ulysses S. Grant at Appomattox Court House.

April 15 Washington, DC Lincoln dies from his wounds.

April 27 Tennessee The Union riverboat *Sultana* sinks on the Mississippi River; 1,400 soldiers on their way home from battle drown.

KEY:

Politics

Land war

Sea war

Virginia. On both occasions, however, Union troops who advanced across the crater caused by the explosion could not get out and became a sitting target. Southern engineers meanwhile dug countermines, or tunnels beneath the Union tunnels, which could then be collapsed or blown up.

Lack of Supplies

For all the bloodshed sieges caused, most ended with defenders being forced to surrender due to starvation. The Confederates at Vicksburg were reduced to eating mule and rat meat by the time they surrendered to Grant on July 4, 1863.

Union troops in the trenches during the Siege of Petersburg. Trench warfare was hard and dangerous. ↓

Siege of Petersburg

For 10 months between June 1864 and March 1865, Grant's troops besieged Lee's Confederate army at Petersburg, Virginia, a vital rail center. Grant built siege lines that extended for 35 miles (56 km). Heavily outnumbered, Lee's troops could not resist. At the Battle of Five Forks on April 1, 125,000 Union troops overwhelmed Lee's 10,000 men. Lee was forced to pull out of Petersburg and retreat. The defeat marked the beginning of the end of his army.

May 10 Georgia Confederate president Jefferson Davis is captured after a surprise raid on his camp at Irwinville.

May 29 The new president, Andrew Johnson, grants an amnesty and pardon to Confederate soldiers, although murderers, arsonists, and others are excluded; former Rebels have to take an oath of allegiance to the US Constitution.

May

May 13 Texas In some of the last fighting of the war, Confederates defeat a small Union force at Palmito Ranch near Brownsville.

Surrender of the Confederacy

General Lee's surrender to General Grant on April 9, 1865, was not the end of the Confederacy. It took several more weeks for the Civil War to come to an end.

Confederate general ≫ Lee signs the document of surrender in the presence of Union general Grant.

Timeline
1865
June–September

June

July

June 2 Texas Having surrendered his army in Mississippi a few days earlier, Confederate general Edmund Kirby Smith flees to Mexico.

July 7 Washington, DC Four people found guilty of conspiracy in Lincoln's assassination—Mary Surratt, Lewis Payne, David Herold, and George Atzerodt—are hanged at the Washington Penitentiary.

June 6 Washington, DC Confederate prisoners of war who are willing to swear allegiance to the Union are released.

June 23 Indian Territory The forces of General Stand Watie become the last Confederates to surrender.

July 21 Massachusetts Harvard University holds a Commemoration Day to honor its war dead.

KEY:

 Politics

Land war

 Sea war

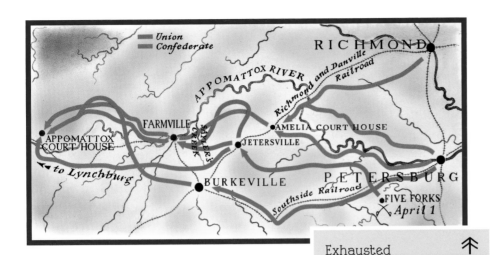

Timeline

April 9, 1865 Talks between Lee and Grant to thrash out surrender terms.

April 26, 1865 Johnston signs new surrender document, acceptable to President Johnson.

May 1865 Most of remnants of Confederacy finally surrender.

June 2, 1865 Jefferson Davis surrenders.

June 6, 1865 Confederate POWs willing to swear allegiance to US are released.

June 10, 1865 President Johnson appoints new governors of Mississippi and Georgia.

June 23, 1865 Stand Watie is last Confederate general to surrender.

August 20, 1866 President Andrew Johnson finally declares the Civil War is over.

Exhausted Confederates struggled west in April 1865 but defeat loomed.

Although Ulysses S. Grant and Robert E. Lee commanded all the Union and Confederate armies, respectively, neither had the political authority to conclude a nationwide peace and end the war. The talks the two soldiers held at Appomattox Court House dealt only with the surrender of Lee's army in Virginia.

Politics of Surrender

President Abraham Lincoln made it clear to Grant that national peace was the sole responsibility of the president. There could be no talks about the surrender of the Confederacy as a nation because Lincoln and his administration had never accepted its claim to be a

September 12 Alabama In the state capital, Montgomery, a convention agrees to restore relations with the federal government.

August   September

September 31 Alabama The state convention abolishes slavery (about 10,000 black Alabamians have fought for the Union army in the war).

The Ceremony of Surrender

On April 12, the Confederate Army of Northern Virginia laid down its arms and battle flags at a ceremony of formal surrender. As the Confederates came down the Union lines, bugles ordered the men in blue to "carry arms," a salute to their enemy which the Southerners responded to in kind. It was a worthy end to the hard-fought war in Virginia.

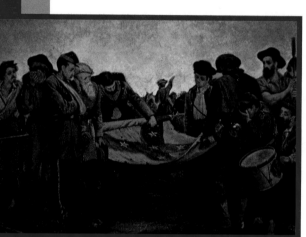

Confederate troops roll up their flag at the formal April 12 ceremony.

Wilmer McLean's house in Appomattox Court House, where Lee surrendered to Grant on April 9, 1865. →

separate country nor recognized the legitimacy of Jefferson Davis's government.

Peace would come when each of the seceded states returned to the Union and accepted the terms on which it was now based, notably the Thirteenth Amendment of January 1865, which abolished slavery. That, however, depended on the surrender of the Confederate armies, which were the only thing holding the South together.

Confederate Surrender

The surrender of the Army of Northern Virginia took three days from the first meeting between Lee and Grant in the parlor of Wilmer McLean's farmhouse in

Timeline
1865
October–December

October   November

KEY:

 Politics

 Land war

Sea war

November 10 Washington, DC Confederate captain Henry Wirz is executed for war crimes committed while he was superintendent of the infamous Confederate prison of Andersonville, where thousands of Union troops died during the war.

the village of Appomattox Court House on April 9. Lee agreed to Grant's written terms.

Lee's surrender left three Confederate forces in the field: the army of General Joseph E. Johnston in North Carolina, that of General Richard Taylor in eastern Louisiana, Alabama, and Mississippi, and General Edmund Kirby Smith's army west of the Mississippi River. Johnston surrendered on April 26, Taylor in early May, and Kirby Smith on May 26. The last Confederates surrendered in Indian Territory on June 23.

Final Capitulation

On June 6, Confederate prisoners of war willing to take the oath of allegiance were released. A few days later, President Andrew Johnson began to appoint governors for the former Confederate states. Despite the rapid move toward peace and reconciliation, it was not until August 20, 1866, that Johnson officially declared the Civil War was over, proclaiming that "The insurrection is at an end."

The Lost Cause

The Lost Cause myth developed among Southerners after the war. It included an idealized view of the Old South, where slaves and masters lived in harmony. It argued that the war was not caused by slavery but by Northern aggression. Against impossible odds, the South had taken up the honorable fight for the states' rights.

← Union general Custer accepts a flag of truce from a defeated Confederate officer, April 1865.

December 18 Washington, DC The US Congress ratifies the Thirteenth Amendment to the Constitution, which abolishes slavery as a legal institution in the United States.

December

Glossary

abolition The ending of slavery; supporters of abolition were known as abolitionists.

artillery Heavy weapons such as cannon and mortars, which can fire large shells long distances.

blockade Measures aimed at preventing trade by using ships to intercept vessels heading toward port.

cavalry Soldiers who go into battle on horseback.

conscription Forcing civilians to join the army: both the Union and the Confederacy used conscription.

counterattack To respond to an attack by launching an attack of one's own.

emancipation Another word for "freedom."

garrison A group of soldiers who occupy a military post.

infantry Soldiers who fight on foot with small arms, as opposed to cavalry or artillery.

ironclad A Civil War ship that was protected by iron armor.

mine A hidden explosive device designed to destroy enemy transportation, such as ships.

mortar A type of short-barreled cannon designed to lob shells over the top of defensive fortifications.

refugees People who have been displaced from their homes by war, starvation, or other disasters.

regiment A military unit that, at full strength, includes 10 units of 100 men; in the Civil War, regiments were rarely at full strength.

secession Breaking away from the Union; states that seceded from the Union formed the Confederacy.

siege A campaign to capture a town or an army by surrounding it and cutting off its supplies.

skirmish A minor fight.

Further Reading

Books

Beller, Susan Provost. *Billy Yank and Johnny Reb: Soldiering in the Civil War.* Twenty-First Century Books, 2007.

Doeden, Matt. *Weapons of the Civil War.* Capstone Press, 2008.

Fay, Gail. *Battles of the Civil War* (Heinemann Infosearch). Heinemann Raintree, 2010.

Golay, Michael. *Civil War* (America at War). Chelsea House Publications, 2010.

Kent, Zachary. *The Civil War: From Fort Sumter to Appomattox* (The United States at War). Enslow Publishers, 2011.

Koestler-Grack, Rachel A. *Abraham Lincoln* (Leaders of the Civil War Era). Chelsea House Publications, 2009.

Miller, Reagan. *A Nation Divided: Causes of the Civil War* (Understanding the Civil War). Crabtree Publishing Company, 2011.

Ollhoff, Jim. *The Civil War* (African American History). ABDO and Daughters, 2011.

Roche, Tim. *Soldiers of the Civil War* (Heinemann Infosearch). Heinemann Raintree, 2010.

Slavicek, Louise Chipley. *Women and the Civil War.* Chelsea House Publications, 2009.

Stanchak, John E. *Eyewitness Civil War.* Dorling Kindersley, 2011.

Westwell, Ian. *The Civil War* (Wars Day by Day). Brown Bear Books, 2008.

Websites

www.civilwar.com
Comprehensive privately run, moderated site on the Civil War.

www.civil-war.net
Collection of images, written sources, and other material about the Civil War.

www.historyplace.com/civilwar
The History Place Civil War timeline.

www.pbs.org/civilwar
PBS site supporting the Ken Burns film *The Civil War.*

www.civilwar.si.edu
The Smithsonian Institution's Civil War collections, with essays, images, and other primary sources.

Index